Sounds and Letters Skills

Level K

Teacher's Annotated Edition

A Division of The McGraw-Hill Companies

Columbus, Ohio

www.sra4kids.com

SRA/McGraw-Hill

A Division of The **McGraw·Hill** *Companies*

Copyright © 2002 by SRA/McGraw-Hill.

Send all inquiries to:
SRA/McGraw-Hill
8787 Orion Place
Columbus, OH 43240-4027

Printed in the United States of America.

ISBN 0-07-570197-9

3 4 5 6 7 POH 07 06 05 04

Table of Contents

Name _____ Date _____

Directions: Find and circle capital letters A, B, C, D, E, F, and G.

Sounds and Letters Skills • *Identifying A–G*

Directions: Find and circle small letters *a, b, c, d, e, f,* and *g.*

UNIT 1 School • **Lesson 14** *Fine Art*

Directions: Write small letters *a–h* under the matching capital letters.

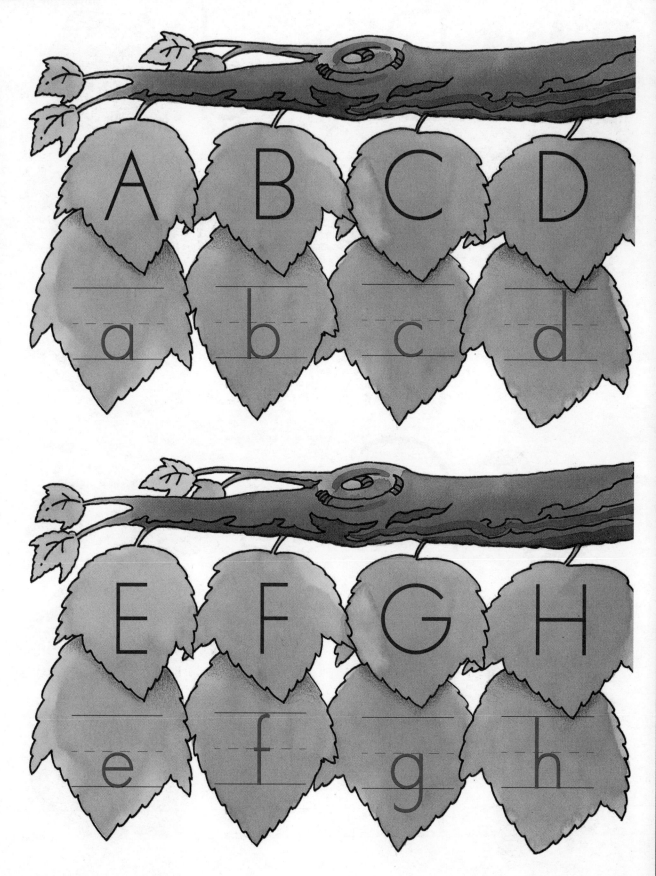

Sounds and Letters Skills • *Writing a–h*

UNIT 1   School • **Lesson 16** *Annabelle Swift, Kindergartner*

B   d

D   b

H   c

C   i

I   h

F —— f

Directions: Draw a line from the capital letter to its matching small letter.

Directions: Circle the small letter that matches the capital letter.

A   c e a ⓐ

E   ⓔ h l

I   j ⓘ l

C   ⓒ o e

K   f b ⓚ

Directions: Connect the dots, in order from A to L, to complete the picture of the bluebird.

Directions: Practice writing the capital and small forms of the letters *Ll, Mm,* and *Nn.*

L L L L L L L L

I I I I I I I I

M M M M M M M M

m m m m m m m m

N N N N N N N N

n n n n n n n n

Directions: Connect the capital letters from *I* to *O* to help the chef reach the pot at the end of the maze.

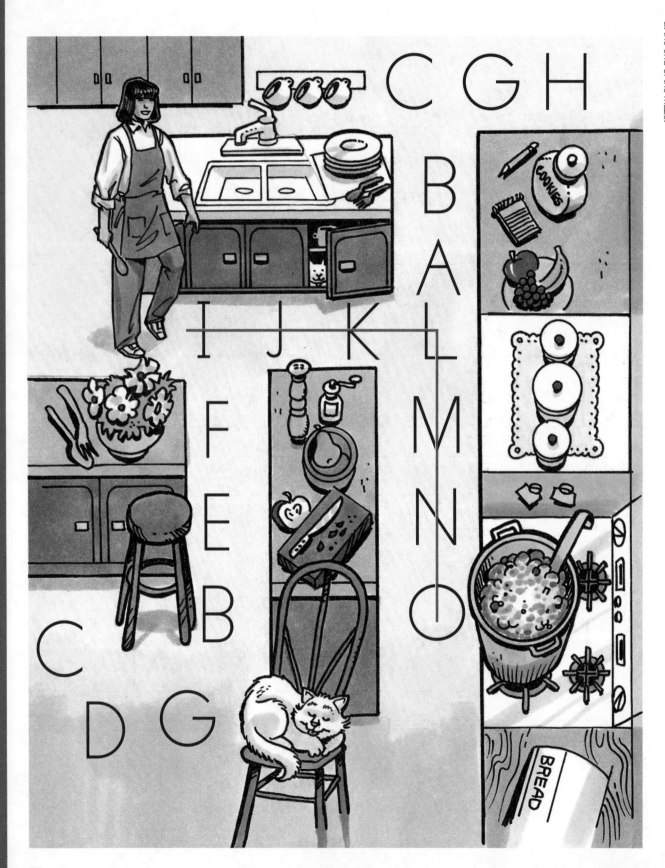

Directions: Circle each capital letter and draw a line to its matching small letter.

h   f   s   m   p   j   t

Ss Ss Ss Ss Ss

Tt Tt Tt Tt Tt

Directions: Write the capital and small forms of the letters Ss and Tt and color the flower petals that match the letter in the center of each flower.

Identifying Ss–Tt • **Sounds and Letters Skills**

Uu Uu Uu Uu Uu

Vv Vv Vv Vv Vv

Directions: Write the capital and small forms of the letters *Uu* and *Vv* and color the flower petals that match the letter in the center of each flower.

t r
u U u b
u c u

V N
b V
P v V
V L

Directions: Circle each capital letter and draw a line to its small form.

Directions: Circle each capital letter and draw a line to its small form.

Sounds and Letters Skills • *Matching Capital and Small Letters*   UNIT 2 • Lesson 14   **13**

UNIT 2 Shadows • **Lesson I7** *Nothing Sticks Like a Shadow*

Directions: Connect the dots, in order from A to M, to complete the picture of the elm tree.

Directions: Connect the dots, in order from *N* to *Z*, to complete the picture of the willow tree.

UNIT 3   **Finding Friends • Lesson 4** *Ginger*

Directions: Circle the small letter that matches each capital letter.

B   (b)   d

D   b   (d)

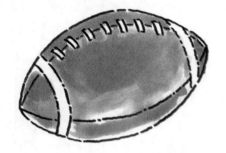

F   (f)   h

H   (h)   b

M   n   (m)

Directions: Circle the small letter that matches each capital letter.

Directions: Circle the word that names the picture.

 map apm

 ent  net

 pins spin

 nam  man

Directions: Circle the word that names the picture.

tab   (bat)

(ham)   mah

anf   (fan)

(bibs)   bisb

 deb

top

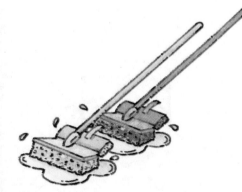 tah

spom

Directions: Circle the word that names the picture.

Directions: Circle the correct word that names the picture.

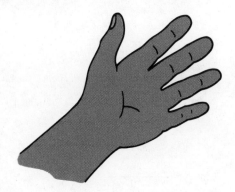

band   hand

bent   dent

pond   fond

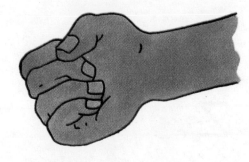

mist   fist

Directions: Fill in the missing letters.

a b c

d e f g h

i j k l m

n o p q r

s t u v w

x y z

Directions: Fill in the missing letters.

A B C

D E F G H

I J K L M

N O P Q R

S T U V W

X Y Z

Directions: Write the capital and small forms of the letter Ss. Write the letter s under the picture whose name begins with /s/.

Ss

S S S S S S S

s s s s s s s

_____   _____

s

Directions: Write the letter s under each picture whose name begins with /s/.

_____
- - - - - - - - - - - - - - - -
_____

_____
- - - - - - - - - - - - S
_____

_____
- - - - S - - - - - - - -
_____

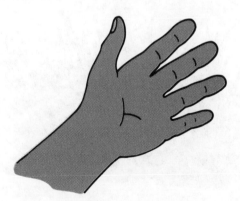

_____
- - - - - - - - - - - - - -
_____

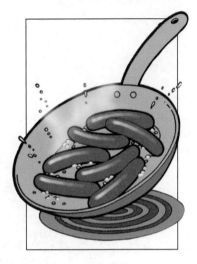

S s

S   S   S   S   S   S   S

s   s   s   s   s   s   s

_____   _____

s

Directions: Write the letter s under each picture whose name ends with /s/.

_____

- - - - - - - - - - - - - - - -

_____

_____

- - - - - - - - - - - - - S - -

_____

_____

- - - - - S - - - - - - - - - -

_____

_____

- - - - - - - - - - - - - - - -

_____

UNIT 4   The Wind • **Lesson 4** *Gilberto and the Wind*

Mm

M M M M M M M M

m m m m m m m m

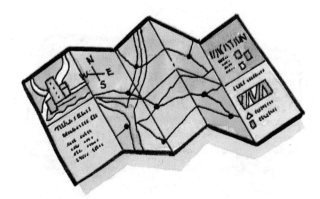

m

Name _____   Date _____

Directions: Write the letter *m* under each picture whose name begins with /*m*/.

m

m

UNIT 4 The Wind • **Lesson 5** *Gilberto and the Wind*

Directions: Write the capital and small forms of the letter *Mm*. Write the letter *m* under the picture whose name ends with /m/.

M M M M M M M M

m m m m m m m m

_____   m

Directions: Write the letter *m* under each picture whose name ends with /m/.

m

_____

m

Name _____ Date _____

S

S

m

m

32   UNIT 4 • Lesson 6   *Identifying Initial Sounds of S and M* • **Sounds and Letters Skills**

Directions: Write *s* under each picture whose name begins with /s/, and write *m* under each picture whose name begins with /m/.

_____

m

_____

s

_____

s

_____

m

Directions: Write the capital and small forms of the letter *Dd*. Write the letter *d* under the picture whose name begins with /*d*/.

Dd

D D D D D D D

d d d d d d d

d _____   _____

Directions: Write the letter *d* under each picture whose name begins with /d/.

d

d

UNIT 4   The Wind • **Lesson 8** *What Happens When Wind Blows?*

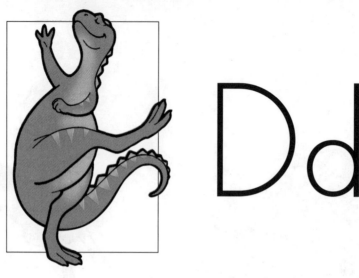

Directions: Write the capital and small forms of the letter *Dd*. Write the letter *d* under the picture whose name ends with / *d* /.

D D D D D D D D

d d d d d d d d

d _____

Directions: Write the letter *d* under each picture whose name ends with /d/.

_____

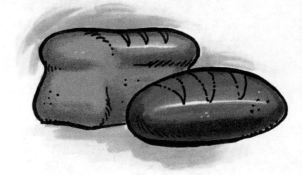

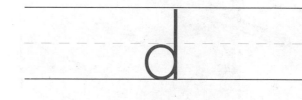

d

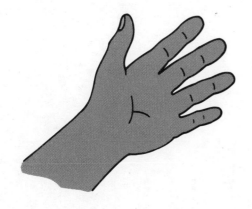

d

_____

Directions: Write *m*, *d*, or *s* next to each picture whose name ends with /*m*/, /*d*/, or /*s*/ to complete the word.

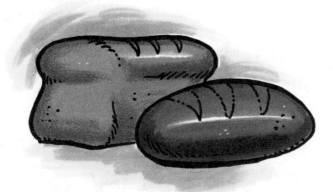

bread

drum

bus

Directions: Write *m*, *d*, or *s* next to each picture whose name ends with /*m*/, /*d*/, or /*s*/ to complete the word.

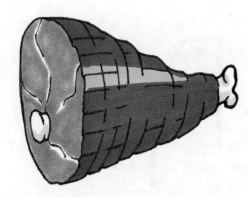

ham

gas

bed

Pp

Directions: Write the capital and small forms of the letter *Pp*. Write the letter *p* under the picture whose name begins with /p/.

P   P   P   P   P   P   P

p   p   p   p   p   p   p

_____   _____

p

Directions: Write the letter *p* under each picture whose name begins with /*p*/.

p

p

Sounds and Letters Skills • *Identifying Initial Sound of P*   UNIT 4 • Lesson 10 **41**

Directions: Write the letter *p* under each picture whose name ends with /*p*/, and write *m* under each picture whose name ends with /*m*/.

m

p

m

p

m

p

Directions: Write the letter *p* under each picture whose name ends with /*p*/, and write *m* under each picture whose name ends with /*m*/.

m

p

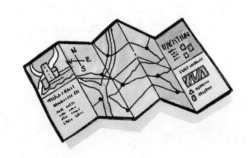

p

m

p

m

Directions: Write the capital and small forms of the letter Aa. Write the letter a under the picture whose name has /a/ in it.

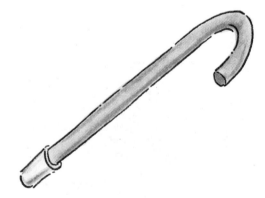

a

Directions: Write the letter a under each picture whose name has /a/ in it.

a

a

a

bat   (cat)

_____

cat

(hat)   pat

_____

hat

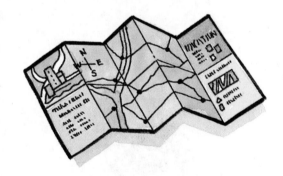

sap   (map)

_____

map

(sad)   pad

_____

sad

Directions: Circle the word with /a/ that names the picture. Then write the word.

Directions: Circle the word with /a/ that names the picture. Then write the word.

 (can)   cap

_____

can

hat   (ham)

_____

ham

jar image

ram   (jam)

_____

jam

fan image

man   (fan)

_____

fan

Directions: Write the capital and small forms of the letter *Hh*. Write the letter *h* under the picture whose name begins with /*h*/.

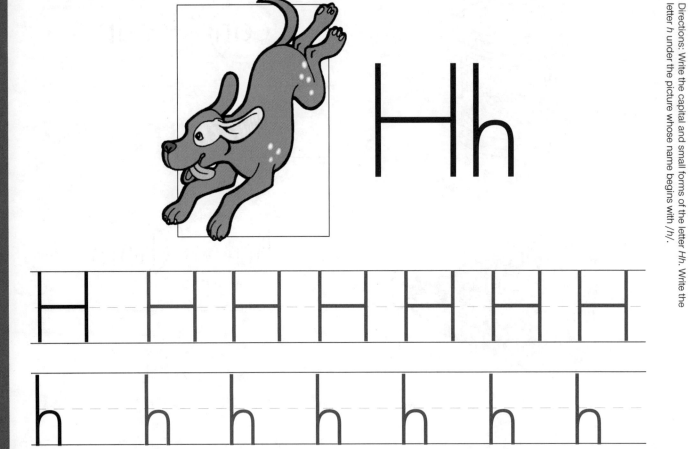

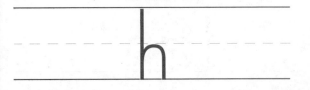

h

Directions: Write the letter *h* under each picture whose name begins with /h/.

h

h

Tt

T | T | T | T | T | T | T

t | t | t | t | t | t | t

Directions: Write the capital and small forms of the letter *Tt*. Write the letter *t* under the picture whose name begins with /t/.

t

Directions: Write the letter *t* under each picture whose name begins with /t/.

t

t

Directions: Write the capital and small forms of the letter *Tt*. Write the letter *t* under the picture whose name ends with /t/.

T T T T T T T T

t t t t t t t t

t _____

Directions: Write the letter *t* under each picture whose name ends with /t/.

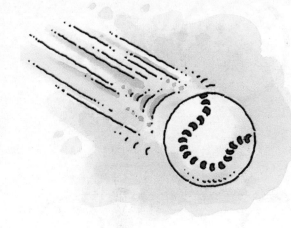

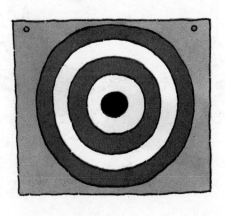

UNIT 4   The Wind • **Lesson 17** *Wind Says Good Night*

Directions: Write the capital and small forms of the letter Oo. Write the letter o under the picture whose name has /o/ in it.

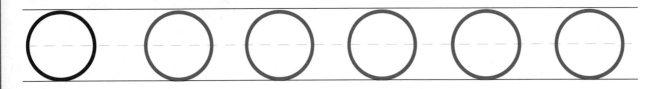

Directions: Write the letter o under each picture whose name has /o/ in it.

(lock)   rock

lock

(mop)   tot

mop

hot   (dog)

dog

(pot)   drop

pot

Directions: Circle the word that names the picture. Then write the word.

Directions: Write the letter o under each picture whose name has /o/ in it.

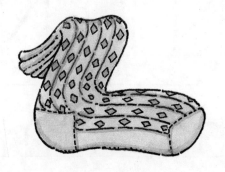

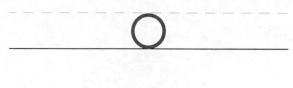

Directions: Write the capital and small forms of the letter *Nn*. Write the letter *n* under the picture whose name begins with /n/.

N N N N N N N N

n n n n n n n n

n _____   _____

Directions: Write the letter *n* under each picture whose name begins with /n/.

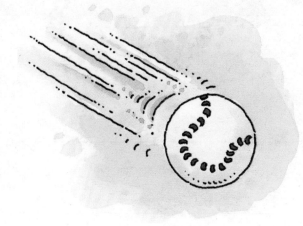

_____

- - - - - - - - - - - - - - - - n

_____

_____

- - - - - - - - - - - - - - - - n

_____

Directions: Write the letter *n* under each picture whose name ends with /n/.

n

n   n

n

UNIT 4   The Wind • **Lesson 20** *Unit Wrap-Up*

Directions: Write the letter *n* under each picture whose name ends with /n/.

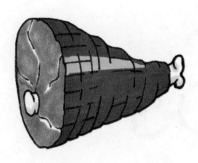

_____

_____

n

n

Sounds and Letters Skills • *Identifying Ending Sound of N*   UNIT 4 • Lesson 20 **61**

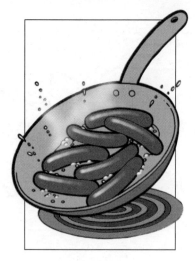

S s

Directions: Write the capital and small forms of the letter Ss. Write the letter s under the picture whose name begins with /s/.

S   S   S   S   S   S   S

S   S   S   S   S   S   S   S   S

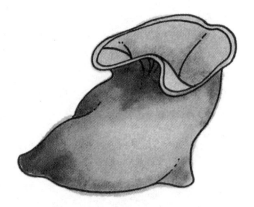

s

Directions: Write the letter s under each picture whose name ends with /s/.

S

S

Mm

M M M M M M M

m m m m m m

_____   _____

m ____

Directions: Write the capital and small forms of the letter *Mm*. Write the letter *m* under the picture whose name begins with /m/.

Directions: Write the letter *m* under each picture whose name ends with /m/.

m

_____

_____

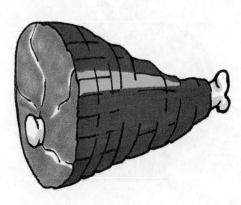

_____

m

Sounds and Letters Skills ● *Identifying Ending Sound of M*　　　**UNIT 5 ● Lesson 4　65**

UNIT 5   **Stick to It • Lesson 5** *The Great Big Enormous Turnip*

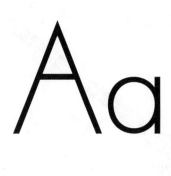

Aa

A A A A A A A A A

a a a a a a a a

Directions: Write the capital and small forms of the letter Aa. Write the letter a under the picture whose name begins with /a/.

a

_____

Directions: Write the letter a under each picture whose name begins with /a/.

a

a

UNIT 5 **Stick to It • Lesson 6** *Tillie and the Wall*

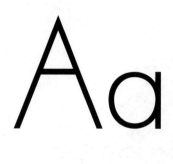

Directions: Write the capital and small forms of the letter Aa. Write the letter a under the picture whose name has /a/ in it.

A A A A A A A A

a a a a a a a a

a

Identifying Short A • **Sounds and Letters Skills**

Directions: Write the letter a under each picture whose name has /a/ in it.

_____

- - - - - - - - - - - - - - - -

_____

_____

- - - - - - - - - - - - - - - -

_____ a _____

_____

- - - - - - - - - - - - - - - -

_____ a _____

_____

- - - - - - - - - - - - - - - -

_____

UNIT 5 **Stick to It • Lesson 8** *Tillie and the Wall*

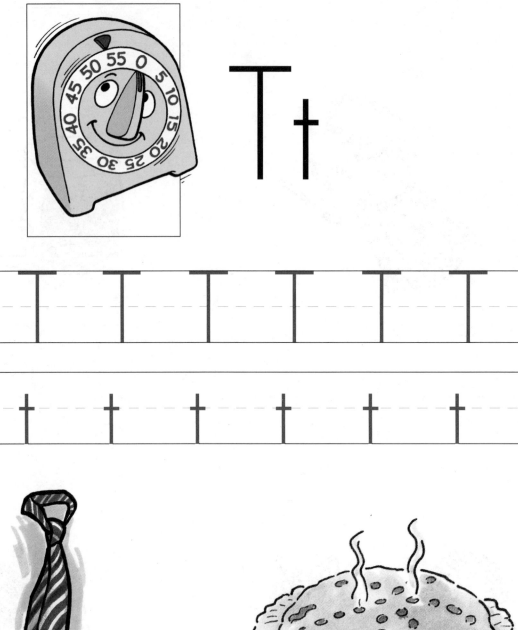

T

t

t

Directions: Write a capital *T* under each picture whose name begins with /t/ and write a small *t* under the picture that ends with /t/.

T

t

T

Hh

Directions: Write the capital and small forms of the letter *Hh*. Write the letter *h* under the picture whose name begins with /*h*/.

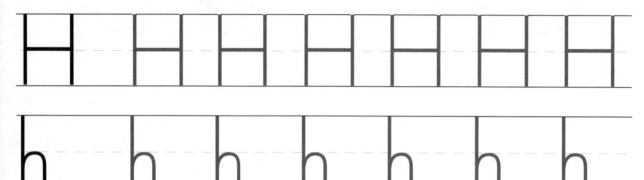

h

h

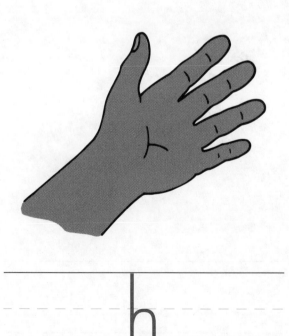

h

Sounds and Letters Skills • *Identifying Initial Sound of H*   UNIT 5 • Lesson 12   **73**

Directions: Write the capital and small forms of the letter *Pp*. Write the letter *p* under the picture whose name begins with /p/.

P   P   P   P   P   P   P   P

p   p   p   p   p   p   p   p

p

Name _____ Date _____

Name _____ Date _____

Name _____ Date _____

UNIT 5 **Stick to It • Lesson 13** *Fine Art*

Directions: Write the letter *p* under each picture whose name ends with /p/.

p

p

Sounds and Letters Skills • *Identifying Ending Sound of P*   **UNIT 5 • Lesson 13** **75**

UNIT 5   Stick to It • **Lesson 16** *Wanda's Roses*

I i

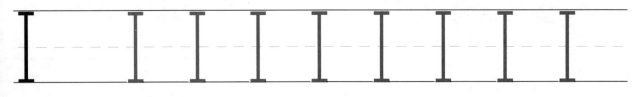

i

Directions: Write the letter *i* under each picture whose name has /i/ in it.

i

i

Ll

Directions: Write the capital and small forms of the letter *Ll*. Write the letter *l* under the picture whose name begins with /l/.

_____   _____

UNIT 5   Stick to It • **Lesson 17** *Wanda's Roses*

Directions: Write the letter *l* under each picture whose name begins with /l/.

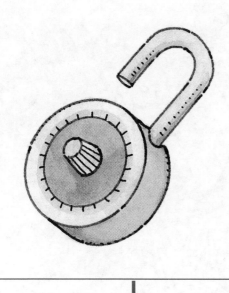

_____|_____
- - - - | - - - -
_____|_____

_____
- - - - - - - - -
_____

_____|_____
- - - - | - - - -
_____|_____

_____
- - - - - - - - -
_____

Sounds and Letters Skills • *Identifying Initial Sound of L*   UNIT 5 • Lesson 17   **79**

Directions: Find and circle all the objects in the picture that end with /l/. Write the capital form of the letter L l.

Identifying Ending Sound of L • **Sounds and Letters Skills**

Name _____ Date _____

Directions: Find and circle all the objects in the picture that end with /l/. Write the small form of the letter *Ll*.

Nn

N N N N N N N N

n n n n n n n n n

Directions: Write the capital and small forms of the letter *Nn.* Write the letter *n* under the picture whose name begins with /n/.

n

Directions: Write the letter *n* under each picture whose name begins with /n/.

n

n

Sounds and Letters Skills • *Identifying Initial Sound of N*   UNIT 6 • Lesson I   **83**

Directions: Circle all the items in the cart that end with /n/. Write the capital form of the letter *Nn*.

Identifying Ending Sound of N • **Sounds and Letters Skills**

Directions: Circle all the items in the cart that end with /n/. Write the small form of the letter *Nn*.

D d

D D D D D D D D D

d d d d d d d d

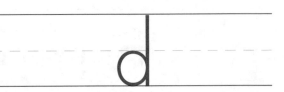

d

Directions: Write the capital and small forms of the letter *Dd*. Write the letter *d* under the picture whose name begins with /d/.

Directions: Write the letter *d* under each picture whose name ends with /d/.

d

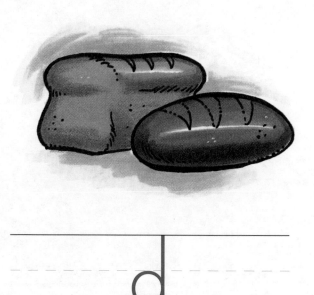

d

Sounds and Letters Skills • *Identifying Ending Sound of D*   UNIT 6 • Lesson 4   **87**

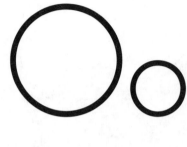

Directions: Write the capital and small forms of the letter Oo. Write the letter o under the picture whose name begins with /o/.

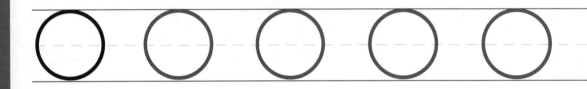

Name _____ Date _____

Directions: Write the letter o under each picture whose name has /o/ in it.

_____

- -

◯

_____

_____

- -

_____

_____

- -

_____

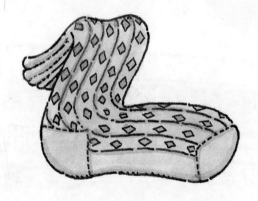

_____

- -

_____

Sounds and Letters Skills • *Identifying Short O*

Bb

Directions: Write the capital and small forms of the letter *Bb.* Write the letter *b* under the picture whose name begins with /b/.

B B B B B B B

b b b b b b b

b

Directions: Write the letter *b* under each picture whose name begins with /b/.

b

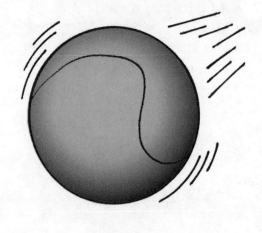

b

Directions: Circle all the pictures that end with /b/. Write the capital form of the letter Bb.

B B B B B B B

Directions: Circle all the pictures that end with /b/. Write the small form of the letter *Bb*.

C C C C C C C C

c c c c c c c

c

Directions: Write the letter c under each picture whose name begins with /k/.

_____

- - - - - - - - - - - - - - - - -

_____

_____

- - - - - - - - - - - C - - - - -

_____

_____

- - - - - - - - - C - - - - - - -

_____

_____

- - - - - - - - - - - - - - - - -

_____

R r

Directions: Write the capital and small forms of the letter *Rr.* Write the letter *r* under the picture whose name begins with /r/.

R   R   R   R   R   R   R

r   r   r   r   r   r   r

r _____   _____

Directions: Write the letter r under each picture whose name begins with /r/.

r

_____

_____

r

r

r

r

Directions: Write the letter r under each picture whose name ends with /r/.

Directions: Write the letter *r* under each picture whose name ends with /r/.

_____

_____

r

_____

_____

r

r

_____

_____

UNIT 6   Red, White, and Blue • **Lesson 15** *America the Beautiful!*

Uu

U U U U U U U

u u u u u u u

u _____

Identifying Short U • Sounds and Letters Skills

Directions: Write the capital and small forms of the letter *Uu*. Write the letter *u* under the picture whose name has /u/ in it.

Directions: Write the letter *u* under each picture whose name has /u/ in it.

u

u

Directions: Write the capital and small forms of the letter Gg. Write the letter g under the picture whose name begins with /g/.

Gg

G G G G G G G

g g g g g g g

_____   _____

g _____

Directions: Write the letter *g* under each picture whose name begins with /g/.

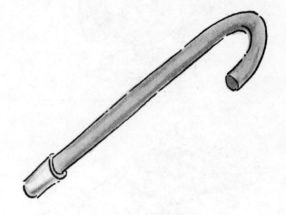

g

g

Directions: Circle the word with the final /g/ that names the picture. Then write the word.

pig   (wig)

_____

wig

(rug)   bug

_____

rug

(pig)   fig

_____

pig

(ladybug)   hug

_____

ladybug

Directions: Circle the word with the final sound of /g/ that names the picture. Then write the word.

log   (hog)

hog

(egg)   leg

egg

hog   (dog)

dog

bug   (mug)

mug

Directions: Write the capital and small forms of the letter *Jj*. Write the letter *j* under the picture whose name begins with /j/.

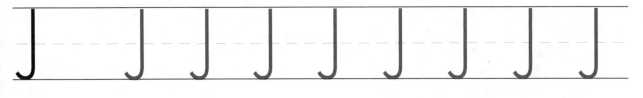

_____

j

_____

Directions: Write the letter *j* under each picture whose name begins with /j/.

j

j

UNIT 7 Teamwork • **Lesson I** *Unit Introduction*

Directions: Write the capital and small forms of the letter *Ff*. Write the letter *f* under the picture whose name begins with /f/.

F f

F F F F F F F

f f f f f f f

f _____   _____

Directions: Write the letter *f* under each picture whose name begins with /f/.

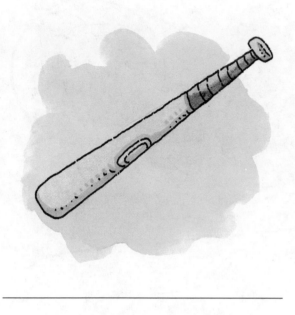

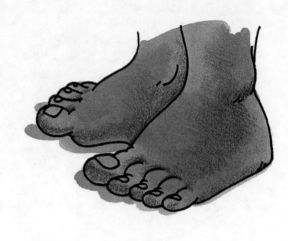

_____

_____

                                          f

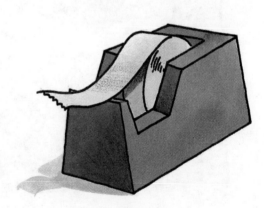

_____ f _____

_____

Name _____ Date _____

Directions: Circle the objects in the picture whose names end with /f/.

f f f f f f f f f f f

Sounds and Letters Skills • *Identifying Ending Sound of F*   UNIT 7 • Lesson 2   **111**

UNIT 7   Teamwork • **Lesson 4** *Team Time!*

E e

Directions: Write the capital and small forms of the letter Ee. Write the letter e under the picture whose name has /e/ in it.

E E E E E E E

e e e e e e e e

_____   _____

e

Directions: Write the letter e under each picture whose name has /e/ in it.

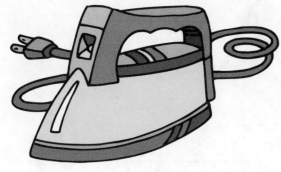

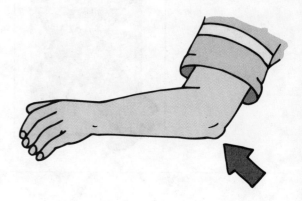

e

e

Directions: Write the capital and small forms of the letter Xx. Write the letter x under the picture whose name ends with /ks/.

X   X   X   X   X   X   X

x   x   x   x   x   x   x

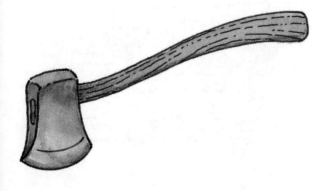

_____   _____

_____ x _____   _____

Directions: Write the letter x under each picture whose name ends with /ks/.

_____

- - - - - - - - - - - - - - -

_____

_____

- - - - - - X - - - - - - -

_____

_____

- - - - - - X - - - - - - -

_____

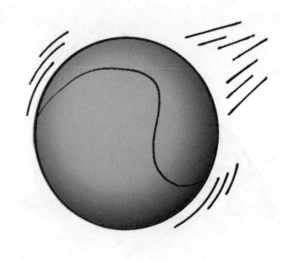

_____

- - - - - - - - - - - - - - -

_____

Name _____ Date _____

UNIT 7 Teamwork • **Lesson 7** *Swimmy*

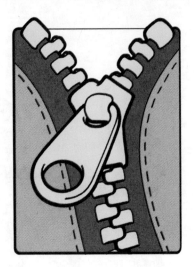

Zz

Directions: Write the capital and small forms of the letter Zz. Write the letter z under the picture whose name begins with /z/.

Z Z Z Z Z Z Z Z

z z z z z z z z

_____   z

116 UNIT 7 • Lesson 7   *Identifying Initial Sound of Z* • Sounds and Letters Skills

Directions: Write the letter z under each picture whose name ends with /z/.

Z

Z

Directions: Tell the students to say each picture name. Then circle the letter in the name that makes the /z/ sound.

ro(s)e

egg(s)

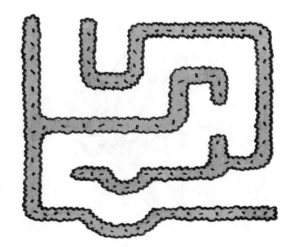

ma(z)e

bla(z)e

Directions: Tell the students to say each picture name. Then circle the letter in the name that makes the /z/ sound.

prize

nose

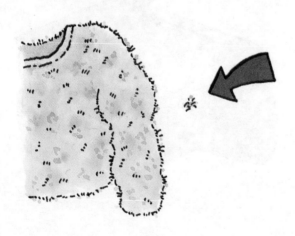

fuzz

wigs

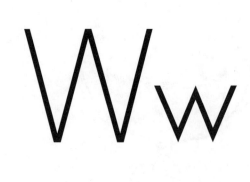

Directions: Write the capital and small forms of the letter Ww. Write the letter w under the picture whose name begins with /w/.

W

Directions: Write the letter *w* under each picture whose name begins with /w/.

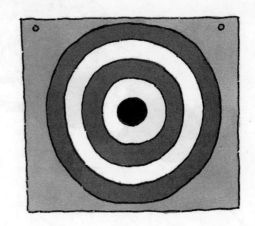

W

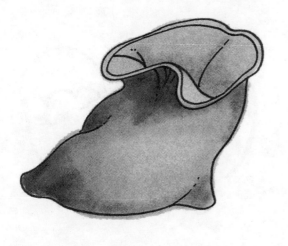

W

Kk

Directions: Write the capital and small forms of the letter Kk. Write the letter k under the picture whose name begins with /k/.

K   K   K   K   K   K   K

k   k   k   k   k   k   k

k   _____

Directions: Write the letter k under each picture whose name begins with /k/.

k

k

Directions: Follow the maze and circle each stone with a picture whose name ends with /k/ to help the King find his bike. Write the capital form of the letter Kk.

Name _____ Date _____

Directions: Follow the maze and circle each stone with a picture whose name ends with /k/ to help the Queen find her book. Write the small form of the letter Kk.

k k k k k k k k k k

Sounds and Letters Skills • *Identifying Ending Sound of K*   UNIT 7 • Lesson 13   **125**

Qq

Directions: Write the capital and small forms of the letter Qq. Write the letter q under the picture whose name begins with /kw/.

Q Q Q Q Q

q q q q q q q

q

Directions: Write the letter *q* under each picture whose name begins with /kw/.

q

q

Yy

Y Y Y Y Y Y Y

y y y y y y y

y

Directions: Write the capital and small forms of the letter Yy. Write the letter y under the picture whose name begins with /y/.

Directions: Write the letter y under each picture whose name begins with /y/.

_____
- - - - - - - - - - - - - - -
y
_____

_____
- - - - - - - - - - - - - - -
_____

_____
- - - - - - - - - - - - - - -
_____

_____
- - - - - - - - - - - - - - -
y
_____

Sounds and Letters Skills • *Identifying Initial Sound of Y*   UNIT 7 • Lesson 17   **129**

Vv

V V V V V V V V V

v v v v v v v v

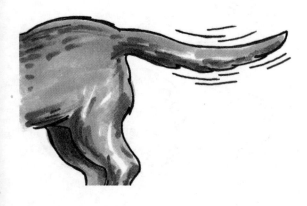

_____   v

Directions: Write the capital and small forms of the letter *Vv*. Write the letter *v* under the picture whose name begins with /v/.

Directions: Write a capital *V* under each picture whose name begins with /v/. Write a small *v* under each picture that ends with /v/.

V

V

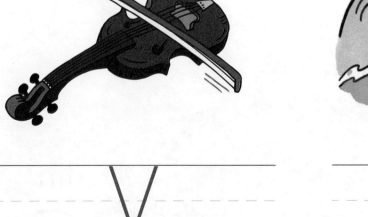

V

V

Name _____ Date _____

UNIT 8   By the Sea • **Lesson I** *Unit Introduction*

Look at the frog _____.

He is on a _____.

The duck sits in the _____.

Directions: Blend and read each word. Then circle the word that completes the sentence.

Identifying Words • Sounds and Letters Skills

Directions: Blend and read each word. Then circle the word that completes the sentence.

Pat can see the _____.

beg

(bug)

Nan sat on the _____.

hit

(hat)

Kim has milk in her _____.

cot

(cup)

UNIT 8   By the Sea • **Lesson 4** *The Ocean*

Directions: Blend and read each word. Then circle the word that completes the sentence.

_____

Here is a _____ for the ham.

(bun)

bin

_____

Will has a bad _____.

lit

(leg)

_____

Mary put a _____ in the wall.

(tack)

tick

Directions: Blend and read each word. Then circle the word that completes the sentence.

_____

Here is a _____.

pin

pond

_____

Mike has a _____.

nap

cap

_____

Do you see the _____?

bug

bag

Directions: Blend and read each word. Then circle the word that completes the sentence.

_____

The lid is on the _____.

pot

mop

_____

Here is a dog in a _____.

wag

wig

_____

She likes to _____.

swim

jump

Directions: Blend and read each word. Then circle the word that completes the sentence.

I wash my hands in a _____.  (sink)
                                              rink

The _____ was in the pond.   luck
                                  (duck)

Dave has a new _____.   (bat)
                              mat

Directions: Blend and read each word. Then circle the word that completes the sentence.

_____

See the ant _____.

(zigzag)

limp

_____

Bees like to _____.

sit

(buzz)

_____

Mom has a big _____.

trip

(van)

138   UNIT 8 • Lesson 9   *Identifying Words* • Sounds and Letters Skills

Directions: Blend and read each word. Then circle the word that completes the sentence.

_____

The _____ is by the farm.

brain
(train)

_____
(lake)

We want to sit by the _____. bake

_____

I see a _____!

(skunk)

trunk

Directions: Blend and read each word. Then circle the word that completes the sentence.

 steps

 slips

The man _____ .

 pan

vat

The egg is in the _____ .

hand

ball

Meg can pitch a _____ .

Directions: Blend and read each word. Then circle the word that completes the sentence.

Stan likes to drink _____.

milk

silk

John ripped his _____.

stuff

cuff

We will _____ the door.

sock

lock

Name _____ Date _____

UNIT 8   By the Sea • **Lesson 14** *Fine Art*

Directions: Blend and read each word. Then circle the word that completes the sentence.

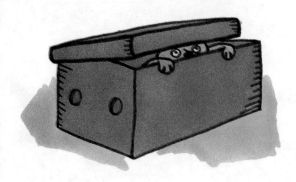

What is in the _____?

fox
(box)

My cat is on my _____.

(socks)
bike

The bear hugs her _____.

(cub)
pup

142   UNIT 8 • Lesson 14   *Identifying Words* • **Sounds and Letters Skills**

Directions: Blend and read each word. Then circle the word that completes the sentence.

The baby is in the _____.

bib

(crib)

The _____ is in her yard.

(stump)

jump

The _____ looked at the dog.

(vet)

bet

Sue has on a _____.

cape

cap

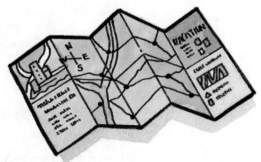

Let's look at the _____.

mat

map

Is the _____ in the shed?

rake

wake

Directions: Blend and read each word. Then circle the word that completes the sentence.

UNIT 8 — By the Sea • **Lesson 17** *Hello Ocean*

Dad likes to _____.

tape

tap

The hen sits on her _____.

nose

nest

kite

quilt

Look at my _____.

Directions: Blend and read each word. Then circle the word that completes the sentence.